Meet the Obamas

America's First Family

By Andrea Davis Pinkney

SCHOLASTIC

New York   Toronto   London   Auckland
Sydney   Mexico City   New Delhi   Hong Kong

Copyright © 2009 by Scholastic Inc.

All rights reserved. Published by Scholastic Inc.,
Publishers since 1920.
SCHOLASTIC and associated logos are trademarks and/or
registered trademarks of Scholastic Inc.

ISBN-13: 978-0-545-20234-3
ISBN-10: 0-545-20234-5

10 9 8 7 6 5 4 3 2 1   09 10 11 12 13

Printed in the U.S.A.   23
First printing, September 2009
Book design by Kay Petronio

Contents

Chapter One

The People's House

The Obamas look forward to moving into their new home as they celebrate in Chicago on election night, November 4, 2008.

On January 20, 2009, the United States celebrated a historic moment with the inauguration of the country's 44th president, and the first African American president, Barack Obama.

On the day of President Obama's inauguration, nearly 100 members of the White House staff packed all of former President George W. Bush and First Lady Laura Bush's possessions, then unpacked all of the Obamas' belongings, in a few short hours. This included their favorite books, the president's collection of neckties, and the family photo album.

That evening, President Obama and his wife, Michelle, attended ten different inaugural balls. Meanwhile, their daughters, Malia and Sasha (short for Natasha), spent their first night in their new home — the White House — having a scavenger hunt and watching movies.

In the Obama household, family comes first. That's why Malia and Sasha's grandmother,

The tradition of the president's kids standing next to him while he takes the oath of office is fairly recent. Bill and Hillary Clinton began it in 1993 with their daughter, Chelsea.

Mrs. Marian Robinson, has chosen to live with the girls and their parents in the White House, also known as the Executive Mansion.

There are 132 rooms at 1600 Pennsylvania Avenue, the Obamas' official address. Even though the White House is home to the Obama family, 15 million visitors come to the 55,000-square-foot mansion each year. Children and grown-ups from all over the world get the opportunity to enjoy the lawns surrounding the

The president and first lady welcome their first visitors to the White House in the Blue Room, the day after the inauguration.

White House, to walk through the halls of the beautiful home, and to sample meals prepared in the White House kitchen.

One of the special attractions for visitors is a brand-new swing set that the Obamas installed

The Obama family encourages boys and girls to try out Malia and Sasha's new swing set, which was installed at the edge of the White House Rose Garden on March 4, 2009.

Each year, youngsters race to the finish line in the White House Easter Egg Roll, a time-honored tradition. Here, the president cheers on an eager egg roller.

as a welcome to the many boys and girls who come to their home. One favorite game is playing hide-and-seek under the swing set's tented roof.

The Obamas host lots of special events and parties at their house. On Easter Sunday, they invite children to participate in the annual White House Easter Egg Roll, a White House tradition that began in 1878 with President

Barack Obama greets children whom he and his family have invited to the White House South Lawn playground.

Rutherford B. Hayes. The first family also sponsors concerts for local schoolchildren, charity events, and community festivals.

Mrs. Obama invited students from a Washington, D.C., elementary school to help her plant the White House kitchen garden.

These activities allow those who live close by, and also citizens of many nations, to share the Obama home, which the first lady refers to as "the people's house."

On April 9, 2009, children from Bancroft Elementary School in Washington, D.C., helped the first lady plant the White House vegetable garden.

Chapter Two

Who Works at the White House?

White House staff members attend a party for head White House florist Nancy Clark on May 22, 2009.

The White House employs many people to help them keep the Executive Mansion running smoothly. About 1,700 men and women are members of the White House staff, doing everything from cooking to answering telephones. There's even an official White House photographer, a librarian, a florist, and a group of professionals who deliver dozens of Christmas trees and wreaths each winter and help the presidential family decorate with thousands of holiday lights and ornaments.

President Obama, White House receptionist Darienne Page, and Vice President Joseph Biden share a laugh outside the Oval Office.

It's very important that the White House staff members work together as a team. Just two days after the inauguration, Mrs. Obama invited the White House workers to join her in the East Room at three o'clock in the afternoon.

A little boy visiting the White House got to meet the president. He wanted to see if the president's haircut felt like his own.

Working at the White House is fun. Here, staff members join a pizza-tasting party in the Roosevelt Room.

There were official White House plumbers, electricians, maids, cooks, and secretaries. Also gathered were men and women who had worked with the Obama family when they lived in Chicago, where Barack Obama served as the junior senator from Illinois before he was elected president. The Obamas invited these professionals to work at the White House, where they are now employed.

The meeting in the East Room included both the new White House employees and those who were already working at the White House when the Obamas arrived. Some of them have served as presidential staff members for many years. The group came together in a big circle around Mrs. Obama, who had called the meeting to introduce everyone. This gave them the chance to get to know one another.

Those who work for the White House serve the first family with dignity and grace. Mrs. Obama says, "They work very hard to make the White House a warm family home and a great presidential residence commanding pride and respect throughout this country and around the world."

The White House kitchen is a busy place. Chefs work many hours to prepare healthy meals for the Obama family and their guests. Here, radishes and lettuce harvested from the White House garden are prepared for a special luncheon.

Chapter Three

Comforts of Home

The Obamas and Mrs. Robinson wave from a White House balcony as they welcome spring.

Now that the Obama family is settled into their new house — and Malia and Sasha have made friends at their new school — they can enjoy their home and the personal touches they've added to make it their own.

In addition to the new swing set, Malia, Sasha, and their parents have lots of cool things at their house, which is perfect for superfun playdates and birthday parties. The White House has a swimming pool, a children's garden, and tennis courts on the South Lawn. There is also a bowling alley, a basketball court, and a horseshoe pit.

One of the most amazing parts of family life at the White House is the private movie theater, complete with its own popcorn cart. That's where Malia and Sasha went to watch movies on their first night in the White House. Now the screening room is a good place for the family to relax.

Holding 3-D glasses, the president cheers while watching the Super Bowl in the family movie theater.

Another great thing the Obamas enjoy together in their home is the food. They have an awesome kitchen, where the White House staff makes their favorite meals — simple, tasty food that's also healthy. The chefs whip up dishes such as spaghetti and tomato sauce with broccoli, and yummy treats like freshly squeezed juices.

President Obama shoots hoops on the White House South Lawn basketball court.

Chapter Four

Bo, the Presidential Pup

Six-month-old Bo wears a lei, the traditional Hawaiian necklace worn for special occasions, to greet the Obamas, his new family.

On election night, November 4, 2008, President-elect Barack Obama promised his daughters they could get a dog, now that he'd won the election.

For months, the Obama family searched for the right puppy. In April 2009, they brought home a six-month-old male Portuguese water dog. Malia and Sasha named him Bo. This special pup was a gift from Senator and Mrs. Ted Kennedy, who have three Portuguese water dogs of their own.

Bo is cute and full of energy. He likes to run and play with the president and his girls. One of his favorite things to do is chew on people's feet! Sometimes Bo presents the first lady with a sock that had been missing. Even though Bo can be naughty at times, he's a very loyal pet. He often greets Malia and Sasha when they come home from school and cuddles with them while they read and relax.

Bo makes the president's brief breaks from work lots of fun, especially when they play touch football together.

Bo sure likes living in the White House. Sometimes he gets so excited that he keeps on playing, even when everyone else is in bed. "One night it was ten o'clock. Everybody was asleep, when we heard barking and jumping around," Mrs. Obama says. "The president and I thought somebody was out there. It was just Bo playing with his ball."

The Obama family has learned that one of the best ways to help Bo behave is to close doors in certain rooms and to give him his own sections of the White House where it's okay for him to play freely. "We try to set him up for success," says Mrs. Obama.

President Obama, Malia, and Sasha on the South Lawn of the White House with Bo.

Chapter Five

Family First

Hand in hand, the first family takes a stroll outside of the White House and shares a special "walk-and-talk" together.

Even though the Obama family has lots to do in running the government, sharing their home with visitors, helping all kinds of people, and taking care of their dog, they still find time for family fun and special moments together.

Barack Obama is a father who likes spending lots of time with his daughters. Even though he's very busy leading the nation, "he's not like play dad," says Mrs. Obama. "He's the guy who has read through all of the Harry Potter books with Malia."

In a note to fellow fathers that appeared in *Parade* magazine, President Obama said, "We need to replace that video game with a book and make sure that homework gets done. . . . In our house, we find glory in self-respect and hard work."

Barack Obama says, "Among the many wonderful things about being president is that

Reading is fun for the Obama family. The first lady and her daughters read stories to a group of children at the White House Easter Egg Roll.

I get to live above my office and see Michelle and the kids every day." The president also takes breaks while working, when he goes to the family sections of the White House to see his wife and daughters.

Sometimes Mrs. Obama, Malia, Sasha, and Bo visit the president in the West Wing (the part of the White House where the president's office is located) during his workday. Mrs. Obama says, "If the kids really need to see him, they can. They're free to walk in. They're welcome wherever they want to go around here."

The president and first lady see their girls off to school most mornings and have dinner with them nearly every evening. They also kiss their children good night at bedtime and tuck them in.

Before he became president, Barack Obama wrote a letter to his girls explaining to them why he has chosen to devote his life to serving others. In the letter, he told them he wanted to make the world a better place for them. His letter said, "I realized that my own life wouldn't count for much unless I was able to ensure that you had every opportunity for happiness and fulfillment in yours." And, his letter told them, "that's why I ran for president: because of what I want for you and for every child in this nation."

President Obama receive thousands of letters from American citizens. He reads ten of them every da

President Obama works in the Oval Office a few
weeks after the inauguration.

On election night, the crowd in Chicago waves American flags as they cheer for the soon-to-be president, Barack Obama.